Preface

Hello my name for the purposes of this book is Mr. Nobody. I'm not a black man, white man, Latin man, Asian man, Indian, or what some refer to as bi-racial man. I'm not Jewish, I'm not gay, I'm not transgender, I'm not in prison, I'm not free, I'm not handicapped, I'm not married, I'm not divorced, I'm not rich, I'm not homeless, I'm not illiterate, and I'm damn sure not stupid. I don't live in suburbs, the ghetto, or a trailer park. I'm not short nor tall according to society's standards. I'm just a man that is nobody to me and if you really think about it I'm nobody to you either. But if I want to get married, or convert to Judaism, or go to prison, or become homeless, or marry a Latin, Indian, Asian, or white women then I will have become somebody. I don't believe in religion, but I believe in the devil and God. I'm not Mormon, catholic, Jewish, Christian, Buddhist, Muslim or any other religion, but if I were I would be somebody. I used to watch the daily news on TV daily and hear about all the things that go on in today's world. I normally would here small tidbits about car crashes, sports, weather, and crime. Occasionally someone is holding a special event that is covered by the media like parades, wine testing event, or something of that nature. Certain things on the news would catch my attention, and some wouldn't. Since I was a kid I have been interested in peace, and why the people in the world do the things that they do. The world seemed so small to me growing up on Southern Ave in Springfield, Ohio. I actually didn't even think I would graduate from high school after I became disenfranchised with education during my senior year of High School. I never thought I would subscribe to a frame of thought of realism, and peace. The peace part of it has been a challenge for me from time to time I have lost sight of my feelings about peace, and violence. I thought I would get a job at a fast food restaurant when I was growing up on the south side of Springfield, have a couple of kids and live happily ever after. But boy the things that I have seen and experienced in life far exceed anything like I thought I would have experienced. I have had a long interesting life in the regards of observing and studying the different folkways, and mores of the world's societies. I started watching cable TV, and surfing the internet and the world became a much smaller place. I now watch Fox news, and CNN on a daily basis. Most things in life I just experience and then move on without looking back. The only area of life that I haven't been able to just put behind me is the separation of the masses of the people in the world that are separated by age, race, gender, religion, handicap, body type, education, economic class, nationalism, political party, convicted criminal, geographical, or any other label or status that we hang on ourselves. Other than growing up in a predominant white neighborhood and dealing with some adversity there, and also being impacted by my upbringing have gotten me to the frame of thought that I have arrived at within a fantasy world of our nation. I keep asking the question why, why, why, why, but I have never gotten an answer or solution other than this is just the way things are. What is the solution to the problems that plague society from all of these areas that I mentioned earlier? People try to help and solve all the icsm's of the world and the religious, and gender differences in the world by talking, understanding, passing laws, brute force, love, and war. How did the world become so separated based on economics, race, gender, sexual choice, handicap, nationalism, politics, and especially religion, and at the same time come together because of these labels. We fight for these labels, and we fight against these labels. People are indoctrinated from birth to adulthood by their experiences, education, politics, popular culture like television, and radio. We are all family, or society Indoctrinated by our peers, and numerous other environmental impacted factors that help brain wash us into the people that we are. Some of us grow out of it, some of us never subscribe to it, and some of us use it to our benefit to get what we want out of life. For example if you are black you are taught at an early age that the police are bad, if you are of a certain religion you are taught that being gay is very bad, some people are indoctrinated that killing others that are different then they are will solve all of their problems. We say things like the American Dream, little white house with a picket fence, married with two kids, six figure salary, and a good education. Wow, where did we learn this from, is it an epiphany or a brainwashed ideology that forgets total happiness over indoctrination and societies acceptance. Now in my opinion all of life's indoctrinations are usually wrong and backwards in thinking as far as common sense goes, but if you throw race, or religion into the mix oh boy instant ticking time bomb. We experience these things in music, movies, education, and all other kinds of institutions. But still no solution; solutions that completely solve the problem. This is not a solution to the problem, and it's not a barrier to the problems of society. So what I did is come up with a world called the 12 clovers. 12 different society's that solve all the problems in the United States of America. What would happen to the United States if we divided up in this fashion, would people then be happy, or would all of society's problems based on differences continue? Just think about all of our ancestors thousands of years ago. They didn't have all of this nonsense; they hunted for food found it ate, got some rest and then repeated their actions. I had a dream and the rest of this book explains this dream in graphic detail.

Contents

Chapter 1-Early Childhood

Pg1-6

Chapter 2-Family Relations

Pg7-13

Chapter 3-Best Friends/the Band

Pg14-21-

Chapter 4-Band Camp

Pg22-29

Chapter 5-The Assault

Pg30-36

Conclusion/Imagination

Chapter 1-Early Childhood

The world has come to a crossroads with violence, employment, housing, marriage, religion and all other everyday things that we go through as human being that bring us together or separate us. So in the year 2050 America has now instituted a non-voluntary program called the clover initiative. This is a program of racial, economic, religion, sexuality, ethnicity, political party, age, weight, and education. The rest of the world refused to activate the clover system at this time but instead wants to wait and see how it works for the United States of America. People can choose whatever sector they want to belong too at age 21, and after the decision is made unless the persons situation changes, and they are accepted into another sector then the decisions are final. The United States has become divided into twelve sectors of living. The twelve sectors are by Religion, Race, Sexuality, Mixed race marriage, criminal record, economics, literacy level, political party, weight, gender identity difference, all others, and handicap. There will be sub sets of each category that is within a category. For example if you are rich and black you will live in the black sector but in the rich black sector. This will be broke down the same way in each sector. If you are not an American Citizen you can apply for a sector and they can either accept you or deny you. If you are caught entering a sector without permission for any reason the penalty is automatic death. You will not be given a trial, or the benefit of doubt the fact that you are there is grounds for you to be immediately executed. All non-American who wish to do business deals with have to do so by computer interaction only, signatures, and handshakes will become of legal nature over the internet. If goods are to be traded, sold, or taken to any other sectors they will be done so by airplane, and then trucked out to the various receivers from the airport by truckers. There will be no person to person contact other than an intellectual, and physical Olympics that take place every five years. The

Olympics can be held anywhere in the world and is to be determined by the usually nature of the Olympic committee. Visitation of family members will be permitted but only for up to 72 hours at which time the American visitors must leave and not be allowed to return for at least 6 months. All who violate the American visitation laws will be executed on site. There will be no marriages, or adaption of children across sector zones. Remember the child at the age of 21 will have the opportunity to join their respective zone based on their beliefs. A polygraph test will be administered by the best FBI agent polygraphist in the world at the age of 21 to determine if the person really wants to, and belongs to the sector that they choose. The initial twelve sectors will be called the American sectors and be numbered from 1 to 12. These sectors do include Alaska, and Hawaii. The Government of the United States with the might of the American military has become a national police force that makes sure the sectors are maintained, but won't govern within the sectors. Each sector will have its own leaders if they choose to do so, and they will be picked based on how that sectors chooses to do so. Kids have no rights until they reach the age of 21, the only rights that they have are basic human rights, the right not to be raped, tortured, mistreated, or abused in any fashion regardless of what kind of views they develop as kids. This way for example gay kids wouldn't be killed by a sector because they don't want their kids to grow up and join the gay sector. Trying to alter, or change a kids thoughts as they approach 21, or trying to bribe them in any way is a sentence of death. If you try to in anyway stop your child from leaving to go to their chosen sector you will be killed immediately. No foreigner from any other country will be allowed to join a sector unless that sector has some life altering reason why. It would have to be something very special like for example the person coming in has found a cure for cancer, or something huge on that level. International marriage to Americans are prohibited for any reason. Trying to change the beliefs in any sector is automatic death sentence. At the outset of the sector being erected twenty foot walls are erected to protect each sector, the sector walls are patrolled by the United States Police force. Unless authorized you are not permitted to fly a private aircraft of any kind at any time without special permission from your sector or zone. Some people refer to the Clover system as sectors, other say zones, it means the same thing. The ground is electrified, if you try to tunnel in you will be electrocuted. If you make it in and are challenged as to what you sector number is and is verified by your eyes, and fingerprints and they do not match you will be executed immediately. If you verbally, or physically try to cause an uproar against any other sector in America the penalty is immediate death. Anyone of the age of 25 or higher can join the Unites States Police as but will only be assigned to your sectors walls. To be a subset police officer you must be at least 27 years old. The reason for the age is because it gives people a chance to mature, and get college out of the way if they want to go to college. All United States officers must have a Bachelor's degree. All subset officers must have at least an associate's degree. There are no exceptions period. There are no extraditions allowed of any kind at any time for anything. All leaders in all sectors, and anyone in the legal field, or educational field must possess a Master's Degree or higher no exceptions. All leaders such as Governors, presidents, commissioners etc.... must have a Master's Degree. Divorces are not allowed unless one of the spouse's life or the kids is in fear of the other. There are video cameras on all walls, parks, bars, restaurants, laundry facilities, gas stations, stores, colleges, inside and out of apartments, and dorms, prisons, jails, hospitals, police property, all houses, dog houses, businesses, and on all streets, in all public buildings, and on every stop sign in the city. There is no privacy other than inside your home; the fourth amendment to the constitution, as well as the second, and eighth amendment no longer exist; no exceptions ever for any reason. There are drones that patrol all sectors, and the borders of the country. Education will be taught as it is now except the sectors will only teach their sectors history as it relates to their people, and the violent history that got the country to where it is with the Clover system. Children will not be indoctrinated by any factor of any society. The children will watch video tapes of each sector at age ten, age twelve, age fifth teen, and age eighteen. Children will have each sector explained to them at various time through their entire life and up close and personal from the age of 18 until the age of 21. If you fail your polygraph you will be required to take it again if you fail it again you go to prison for five years in that sector, after five years if you fail again you are executed. None of these things are negotiable, or can be countermanded under any circumstance. The rest of this book will be about the lives of two citizens that were brought together by fate. These two families lived in the working class Christian straight multicultural section of the United State of America. This particular section of the United States was located in the States of Arizona, Utah, Colorado, and Nevada. There are ten sectors that have four states a piece, and two states that consists of five states. On June the 12th, 2050 two special kids were born into the world. Brian and Lisa Brennan are the parents of a baby boy, he was born in Phoenix, Arizona at 12:00PM on the dot; his parents named him Alan. On the same day at the same time a baby girl was born; her parents are named Debbie, and Mathew banter, her parents named her Christy. This was a weird coincidence that Alan grew up in the same neighborhood as Christy. They only lived four houses down from each other. These two kids went to the same elementary school and quickly became friends at the tender age of three. They played with their baby blocks together, and their other toys. They both would eventually attend each other's birthdays for their entire infancy and teen years. Alan was a great kid; always smiling, happy and enjoyed every aspect of his young life. Alan liked to play video games, chess, and checkers, eat junk food, and hang out watching videos with Christy. At the age of six both made a pinky swear that they would be friends forever, and always be there for each other. Their parents even hung out together on some of the holidays like the 4th of July, and Labor Day. They would cook out and roast hot dogs, hamburgers, and chicken wings. They would drink ice cold lemonade and tell each other about what kind of months they had the months before the holiday. Christy and Alan would listen to their parents talk intently about their jobs, and the extracurricular activities. They would wonder what certain things were that they would hear about like rush hour traffic, and happy hour at the local neighborhood bar. At six years old the days were long and drawn out and made the kids look into the sky and wonder about their futures with awe. Not a care in the world or a bad thought entered into either one of their heads. They both were simply six year old kids living their lives to the fullest in their tiny little minds. At the age of seven more of the same followed, family, and friend picnics, and lots of food and ice cold drinks to wash it down with. They used to talk about what they wanted to be when they grew up not realizing the pending possible separation that awaited both of them. Christy wants to be a doctor when she grows up, and Alan wants to be musician of some kind. Alan and Christy became really good friends as kids. They were never boyfriend and girlfriend but they were always there for each other as they grew older. They went to the same junior high School, and eventually the same high school. They always made sure they attended each other's birthday parties even though their birthdays were on the same day. They both liked to same kind of music, activities like camping, and going roller skating. Their favorite color was brown, and they both loved Twinkies, and apple pie. Both of their families were notorious for having cook outs and then having Twinkies, or apple pie as dessert. As the two kids got older their parents separately started explaining to them about America's different sectors of life. Christy was shocked, but Alan understood and thought it was a good ideal that everyone could and would live with people who thought, dressed, talked, walked, and lived the same way that he and everybody else did in their sector. Christy being to over and ultra-caring type thought that she could function anywhere. Christy really enjoyed making other people happy, and thought it would be great as a doctor to be able to care for everyone. She always thought she would live in a city close to the Pacific Ocean, with her husband, kids, pet dog, and cat that she wanted in her adult life. She dreamed about the perfect family and the perfect circumstances that come with life. She wanted to live the dream that she had in her head as a kid. Alan just wanted to go with the flow, he didn't believe in any parameters in his life. He had no intention of going to college, or getting a job working 8 to 5 by any stretch of the imagination. He was a free bird as a kid and wanted to remain that way for the entirety of his life. It is amazing that at such a young age they both knew exactly what they wanted to be when they grew up. They both had dreams about their future lives as far as having a family and the type of life style they wanted. This was all pretty weird considering that as kids they love the same stuff, and absolutely adored the other and hanging out with the other one for hours upon hours. As they approached the tender age of thirteen their lives and who they are stated to take form in the realization that one day they would have to make some very heavy decisions about their futures. Alan was at the age where he was starting to develop feelings for other people as far as relations and being attracted to other kids. Alan had several friends that lived in his neighborhood that were into music like he was. One day he and some other kids decided to form a childhood band; they would call themselves 8 deep. The band consisted of Alan and six of his guy friends that lived in the neighborhood. Three of the kids were white, 2 were black, 1 Asian, and 2 Mexicans. They would meet two times a week after doing their choirs, and eating dinner to rehearse and play for fun. They covered a lot of rock music that they heard on the radio, and they also came up with several songs that they wrote together. They were actually very talented for their ages. No one in the band was over the age of thirteen. They decided they would eventually put on neighborhood gigs at the park, and in their friends back yards when possible. It was spring and summer was quickly approaching. The band members thought it would be a good idea to go to summer band camp together. They would find a private band camp and that way they could hone the skills in together and become a better band then they already were. They chose a camp located in Northern Utah. The trip was a seven hour drive from where they were in Arizona to the camp in Utah. So they went off to band camp for three weeks. They were taught how to do things like build fires from scratch in nature, safe hiking, and enjoying the great outdoors. In the evenings since it was a band camp; the campers would split up into groups and sample music, play music, and listens to others music. One night Alan and one of his new friends that he had met at band camp named Aaron decided to go for a long walk on a beach that was adjacent to the band camp lodge area. As they were walking and talking Alan began to examine how he felt at the moment as far as life and the immediate moment, Alan thought to himself this is great and is how I want to spend the rest of my life. Just nonattached to anything as far as society's structure and the whole rat race of having a 8 to 5 existence and a quote unquote normal life. Aaron said to Alan isn't this wonderful man we are thirteen years old and don't have a care or worry in the world, why can't it always be like this, just plain existence with no parameters of anything holding us back or holding us down? Aaron ask Alan if he had his eyes on any of the female campers and Alan said no, not yet anyway. I don't feel any sparks or attraction to any of the young girls in the band camp. Aaron replied my father told me that I would start to have feelings and getting certain urges as I approached teen hood. Alan replied my father told me the same thing but so far I don't feel anything. I don't even know if I'm ready for a relationship at my age and the way I feel about life right now. Aaron said I'm with you brother let's just enjoy our childhood and live life to its fullest. The two boys headed back to camp and joined the others at their extracurricular activities. Alan was a little home sick so he decided to call Christy to see how she was doing and how her summer was progressing so far. Alan had a cell phone with unlimited text, and minutes so he could talk to Christy for as long as she wanted to speak with him. It was a little after 8:00PM when Alan decided to phone Christy. Christy answered her phone with a vivid excitement after seeing that it was Alan that was phoning her on her caller ID. Hey Alan; how are you doing, are you enjoying camp tell me all about it. Alan excited also, said hey Christy I miss you first of all, and can't wait to get back home and share my experience with you. I love this camp so far, it is so liberating from a freedom standpoint. There is nothing out here except quiet, the animals, and bunch of other great kids who all seem to be out here relaxing and trying to figure out who they are as people. I just came back from long walk with a friend that I made named Aaron, he and I were discussing girls, are feelings, and how good we felt about being here. Christy laughed; you were discussing girls huh, I guess you are maturing into a young man that will have urges, and start growing into a strong family man that I think you will end up being. Yep, Alan says with a funny feeling about talking to Christy about beginning to like girls. I have learned some new songs, and the band is getting a lot better than we were just a month ago. Out here there is no one to bother with our loud playing of our instruments. The animals scatter when we start playing in the evenings, but I think they are getting used to us. Well enough about me what have you been up to? Well I have been also thinking about life in general a lot. I have been thinking about how I can obtain all the things in my life that I want to obtain from a universal standpoint in a society that no longer allows me to be universal. I want so much to serve society in a huge and academic capacity as a great doctor. I want to grow up and get married to my dream man. Oh Alan he will be a great father, head of our family, compassionate about society as a I am, and very smart from an academic stand point and an awe inspiring life standpoint as far as knowledge goes. Wow, Christy you are not asking for a lot are you. Well Alan I know what I want, but getting it will be the long journey and difficult part. Where do you see yourself at in ten years Alan? Christy I don't know where I will be, and don't care as much as where I am as far as my feelings about complete freedom and not being pigeon holed by anyone about how I live my life. Right now I would be happy to get up and walk around all day, and then go play music at night. I don't have the same feelings about family like you do Christy, or at least not now anyway. I understand my friend, but listen Alan we are only thirteen years old. We have plenty of time to get on the right track if we are even on the wrong one. I think we will in time figure out what our young feelings mean and what they are telling us. I know one thing for sure regardless of where I end up I always want you to be a part of my life. I don't care if we both end up on opposite sides of the country. I know that in you have a great friend for life and I don't ever want to lose this feeling that I have about our young relationship as teenagers. Dang girl, I had no idea that you had such strong feelings for our friendship as I do. I feel the exactly the same way about you my friend. I'm glad I called you Christy you always make me feel so happy. All, you make me feel happy to Alan; this is why I like and adore you so much. Maybe we are so close because we were born on the same day in the same place. Maybe our lives were meant to be intertwined, Gemini's forever, ha ha. Yeah Christy I think you may be right, what else have you been up to this summer? Have you started reading the medical books that we used to talk about when we were eleven years old? How are you mother and father doing, and everyone else in our neighborhood? Well my parents are doing fine Alan, everyone in the neighborhood seems to be doing ok. Everyone is happy because of course except for kids they all think alike. So within our living sectors unless people are lying to each other I guess grown adults will never have any problems other than ones created by their children. Yeah I guess that was a dumb question, ha ha. You are not dumb Alan and that was not a dumb question. It's just the fact that we are kids living in someone else's world right now. Our time will come and then ultimate insight and happiness will run its natural course for us as adults. We should not try to grow up to quick as teens. I think we should just enjoy ourselves right now, and enjoy being with our family's everyday if we choose to be. Things will change and then we may look back one day and say if I knew now what I knew then. You are so smart Christy for your age, and in general. You are going to make a great doctor. Your husband is going to be a very lucky man. He will lay beside you one night in bed and tell you that he hit the human sweepstakes when he found you. Thank you Alan that's sweet of you to say. I know that life has some great things in store for us both. Well

Christy they all calling me over to the main tent so I'm going to say bye for now. You have a great night and I will call you again next week and we can resume this heart felt conversation my friend. Ok Alan have a great night yourself kid, and tell all the other band members I said hi. Ok bye for now Christy. Alan returned to the camp and began practicing his craft with his other band members. He kept thinking about what Christy had said and thought wow, I should just enjoy my teen years and worry about adulthood when it gets here. The summer came and went pretty quickly for both Alan and Christy. Alan had learned a lot more about music over the summer, and Christy had read several books about medicine over the summer. They both had fully determined what they wanted to be when they grew up. There was no longer any doubt in either one of their heads. Christy knew that she wanted to be doctor and nothing else, and Alan absolutely positively knew he wanted to be a professional Musician. School was very interesting to Christy because she is such an intellectual being, but Alan feels like school is a waste of his time. Alan doesn't feel like he is learning anything that he will use later on in life other than the social contacts that he is currently making with other classmates that are into music. Being in the eighth grade was not particularly appealing to either Alan or Christy. Although both couldn't wait to experience high school because they both have heard about all of the fun they were going to have doing things like engaging in debate club, or key club for Christy, and for Alan joining the high school band and jamming during band class during the day, and after school at band practice. So life continued on through school year but with one big twist in this year of their life. One day the entire student body was assembled in the Junior High School auditorium. The teachers told the students that they were there to watch a video about the sectors. Everyone sit in silence not knowing how to feel or what to feel as the film started. The film started with images of every country and every race of people on all continents showing any all footage of torture, war, famine, riots, videotaped murders, assassinations, racist rants, and people saying or demonstrating about all the things and people that they hate. People being beheaded, burned at the stake, hanged, stabbed, shot, blown up, and beaten to death. For two hours all of the kids watched videos of Adolf Hitler ranting about Jews, Mussolini ranting about Jews, cars and buildings being blown up, people being shot in war videos, video of the holocaust survivors weighting 50 and 60 pounds, video of lynching's in America of blacks, dogs being sicked on people. Cars running people over, people being beaten on film in bar fights, and street fights, and shootouts with the police or warring enemies in war videos. Even videos of baby's and young kids being kids when bombs have gone off in buildings, and cars, and kids and baby's being killed during drive by shootings from gang members. The kids sit in stunned silence after watching all of these things for two hours straight. Christy who was sitting about four rows over from Alan, looked over at him at the same time he looked at her. She had tears in her eyes and he had a bewildered look on his face about what they had just watched. One of the school teachers took the stage and started to explain about how these things that we had just watched had been completely banned, and given up in our sectored society. She said that we would never again experience a society where two man walking down the street holding hands would be attacked, where someone black would be denied access to a restaurant or hotel because the color of their skin, where someone would shoot the other person because they were in a gang that had a problem with this persons gang, no glass ceiling with pay for a women versus a man for doing the same job. No more calling people racial names, no more creating neighborhood or community's that would discriminate based on religion, creed, height, weight, or any of class or category that we can think of. Essentially the zones had erased hatred based on separation and common living based on who we are what we choose after we are born. The penalty in every zone for even calling someone a discriminating name listed in the United States Code of honor book is punishable by automatic 5 year jail time. No trial, no I'm sorry, no chance for redemption, simply automatic 5 year jail period, unless you are a kid. The teacher told everyone that they knew it was tough to watch all of the violence, death, and sorrow, but imagine having to live it. This assembly is dismissed kids try and enjoy the rest of your school day and always remember that peace by separation is the rule of the nation. Christy passed Alan in the hallway on their way back to classes and asked him if he was ok. Alan answered in monotone voice, I'm fine, just a little taken back by what I just saw. I have never seen violence, or anyone get killed before. No one in our born sector is violent of course, and there is no violence on Television, or even verbally on the radio. So I felt a little queasy watching all of these atrocities take place. I can't believe human beings used to act like this, are ancestors were freaking crazy. I agree with you Alan these films are very disturbing and hard to watch, even harder to comprehend that these things actually took place. Well Alan I will talk to you after school have a great rest of your day. At the end of the school day Alan met with his band friends to practice their music. They all decided because they were depressed that they would write and perform a song dedicated to peace, the song is called "Eclipse of Love". They practiced for two hours in Randy one of the band member's garage. Christy eventually showed up to listen and urge the band on with their practice. They decided to play their new song for her to see if she liked it. When they were finished she was teary eyed and said that she loved the song. She said it made her feel all warm and fuzzy inside.

Chapter 3-Best Friends/the Band

They were all tired and decided to call it a day. Alan told Christy that he would walk her home. As they were walking down the street they found themselves talking again about their lives as they grew older. Christy asked Alan if he had given any thought at all to going to college. Alan said that I thought about it but he felt that is would put shackles on my freedom. I need to be free to roam, and come and go as I please. I don't like to read books and study like you do Christy. I don't like homework and I get bored very easily if I have to stay in the same place for any extended periods of time. I will play it by ear and decide when I'm 17 years old. Christy said that you better make up your mind. You don't want to try and decide at the last minute and then can't get into good school. Alan said ok and told Christy good night as they had reached the front of her house. Alan went home and practically stayed up all night thinking about his life and the future. The film about the world had really made an impact on his psyche and he didn't know how to process his feelings. He thought about waking his mom or dad up and discussing it with them but he didn't. Alan went to school the next day and the memory and visions of the violence slowly disappeared from his frame of thought. The school year went by pretty quickly and Alan Christy found themselves heading into summer at the tender ages of 14. Both of them had plans to basically do what they had done last summer. Hang out with their families having movie nights, cook outs, and with Alan again going away to band camp. Their two family's celebrated their birthdays with a huge cookout and invited all the kids in the neighborhood, and all of their family that still lived in their sector. They ate cheeseburgers, hotdogs, nachos, potato salad, and a huge double birthday cake of course for the main course. There was plenty of ice cold lemonade, and punch. As well as ice cold adult beverages for the adult guest. This party went on into the wee hours of the night. No one complained about the music or loudness because everyone in the neighborhood attended the party. Both Alan and Christy thought wow, we are just four years from being full blown legal adults. Two weeks later Alan returned to band camp once again with his neighborhood band friends. Alan was happy to see his friend Aaron once again, and all of the other teens that had returned to the camp for another summer of music, and outdoor fun. After a couple of days everyone was once again settled in and looking forward to whatever came their way in the form of fun or music. Something totally strange, life changing happened to Alan one night why he was taking a shower in the boys shower room. The shower are communal and big enough to fit 30 or 40 teens in at a time. They were big square shower room that one might find in a huge commercial Gym, or Athletic arena of some sort. Alan was showering and just happened to catch a glance of a pair of eyes that were looking at him from off in the distance of the corner of the shower room. Alan thought to himself maybe someone was lost or just shy about coming in why he was in there so he didn't give it any more attention and returned and finished showering. Later on that evening Alan and Aaron went for a walk to talk about music and just have one of their teen friendship moments like they had shared the summer before. Alan and Aaron talked to each other about how their school years had gone, and what they learned and experienced during the school year. The conversation quickly turned to females, and Aaron asked Alan if he had a girlfriend, or if there was someone that he was interested in. Alan replied no, and asked Aaron if he had a girlfriend and he said no. When Aaron said no he just happened to look Alan in the eyes and Alan into his eyes. Alan got a weird, but warm feeling about the way Aaron glanced at him, but he didn't know how to process the feeling so he just brushed it off as a weird vive. They continued their friendly discussion a little while longer and then returned to camp to join the others for a good old jam session. All the camp teens played, talked and had fun for the next three hours before turning into for bed. The next day after dinner Alan got in on a pickup game of flag football with some other teens. Afterwards they all were pretty dusty and dirty and needed a shower. Alan was the last teen to get back to the camp locker room area and therefore the last one to enter and take a shower. He has this great big shower room all to himself. As he was showering a weird feeling came over that made him feel like someone was watching him. He decided to rinse the lather out of his eyes and turn around as quick as he could and sure enough he just caught a glance of another teen that he was pretty sure was Aaron that was looking at him. At that moment Alan had the same feeling that he had when he and Aaron had made contact the night before taking their friendly little walk. Alan didn't know how to process how he felt at this moment as far as feelings go, but he knew he wasn't mad and he didn't understand why he wasn't mad. Why would Aaron be trying to watch him take a shower though, why wouldn't he say something, why would he just linger in the distance trying watching him. Alan finished his shower and went to bed without thinking about it any longer that evening. The next day at breakfast Aaron would not make eye contact with Alan and sit on the other side of the cafeteria pretty much acting like he didn't know Alan. Later on that day Alan walked up to Aaron and asked him if he would take a walk with him so that they could talk. Aaron reluctantly said yes with a little tremor in his voice and off they went. Alan said dude I saw you checking me out when I was in the shower last night, I was wondering why you did that. Aaron said with a strong tremor in his voice that I think I'm gay. Last summer hanging around you I had some feelings that popped up, and then this year I just haven't been able to contain them. Aaron you are only fourteen years old

Alan replied, how do you know that you are gay? Aaron replied again with his voice becoming even shakier, that I have known all of my life, I have never liked females at all in fact I find them in different in the fact that I can be friends with them but nothing else. Well I don't feel the same way Aaron I'm pretty sure that I like girls. Aaron replied have you ever had a girlfriend. Alan explained that he hadn't ever had a girlfriend in the sense of my kiddy relationship or crush, but he does have very good female friend named Christy that he grew up with. Aaron asked well do you have feelings for her. Alan said no but I feel like we are very close. I can talk to her about anything and vice versa, we share everything with each other including family events, birthdays, and anything else that people do together. I must admit that I'm not mad at you for it, but I don't think that I'm gay dude. Ok, well Alan does this mean that we are not friends anymore. No Aaron if you want to be we are still friends, your sexuality doesn't mean a lot to me because we are kids anyway. So as teens even if you were a girl we are only 14 years old. Yeah, Alan you have a point; and by the way can we keep this between us I don't want to get hassled by the others kids in the camp. Ok, I won't say a word Alan replied but I don't want to catch you watching me showering again, it's not cool. Ok, deal I will not try to look at you anymore why you are showering, but I still think you are a nice guy and I think that is why those feelings came out. You are one of the few people that I know that actually listen to me and seem to be genuine person. Even if I have only known you for a couple of weeks from last summer and this summer. You are a cool kid and I hope we are friends for a very long time, or at least until we have to pick our sectors at age 18. They went back to band camp and started jamming out with their bands. The night progressed on and either one of them gave another thought to what had happened with the showers, and about their little talk. The next day went on without any indifference to anything. The kids engaged in all types of activities from painting to playing volleyball and a lot of other games. Later on that evening Aaron went to go take a shower, as he entered the shower room he noticed that he was the only one in the shower. He lathered up and began taking his shower. He got a lot of soap in his eyes, and turned sideways so that the water would hit him just right to get the soap off of his face, and to his complete amazement he saw a figure off in the distance looking at him. But as soon as he turned that way the figure quickly disappeared. Aaron was actually scared now and cut his shower short. He thought what kind of pervert would be watching him shower. But then he thought wow that is the same thing that he did to Alan. Aaron said to himself that I guess I deserved that after what I did to Alan, but I wonder who that was. I hope it wasn't one of the camp counselors that wouldn't be cool. Aaron went back to his lodge and lay in bed drifting off to sleep trying to figure out who would want to watch him take a shower. Then he thought Alan, but Alan said that he isn't gay, and that what I did was not cool so it couldn't have been him right. The next day Aaron didn't say anything to anyone he just went on with his normal camp day. The next couple of weeks went by pretty quickly and everyone said their goodbyes and went home. Once back at home Alan told his best friend Christy one day about what happened at band camp. Christy laughed and said if I was in camp I must say I may have tried to steal a little peak of you showering myself. They both laughed hysterically about it and thought oh well these things are just part of life. The next school year came and went without much changing in anyone life. As the school year was fast approaching Alan, and Christy both started to realize and experience certain physiological changes in themselves. Christy got her period for the first time and was totally freaked out. Her mother explained to her that this is part of human nature and it just means that she is becoming a young woman. Christy immediately went to the library and read every book she could find about young women having their periods and what this meant. She was shocked, but also amazed at how the human body works. Alan on the other hand was starting to grow a mustache for the first time in his life. Alan felt pretty good about being able to start the buddings of a mustache. They both decided to have a movie night and discuss the changes that they were going through as young adults. They both picked a movie that they wanted to see and met at Christy house to watch movies, talk, and eat nachos, and drink cold lemonade. Christy told Alan that he looked sexy with his budding mustache, he laughed and replied that he thought he looked like Tom Sellick. Alan asked Christy how her life was going and how was everything going. Christy told him that she got her period and that she felt like they were quickly approaching adulthood. Christy told Alan that for the first time in her life she didn't feel like a kid anymore. Christy explained that not only was her body changing but the way she felt about politics, people, and life in general were changing also. Christy said that she didn't feel the same way anymore about patriotism, freedom, money, and a lot of other things in life. Alan said that he felt the same way. Alan said that he didn't want to leave his parents and go to another sector but that he was pretty sure that the one they were in didn't fit his personality. Christy said with me we will have to wait and see I think I may be staying here by all accounts I'm a working class, white Christian with moderate views. As they continued to watch the movie sleepless in Seattle Alan thought I can't believe in three short years all whole world will be turned upside down. Why doesn't the United States have plan of life where you actually get to live a little before you have to make a decision about what you want to really do, and go with our lives. Christy laughed and said they do its call childhood, and being a teenager. Well Alan replied it's too quick for me, I haven't even decided what my priorities are yet. Christy replied that she had done some research about how society used to be and that when they waited people just became more uncivilized and violent as they tried to find the niche in life. The Government came up with this plan when they realized that we were about to destroy ourselves from the inside out. We were about to make ourselves extinct based on our views, beliefs, indoctrinations, and icsms. What are icsms Alan asked? Christy explained that icsms are racism, sexism, ageism, fatcism, and any other ways of being mean to a group of people can be termed. Why couldn't are predecessors get along Christy? Why were they so engrossed in life and their family to be worried about what other people were doing, or how others were living their lives? I don't know, and I don't know why they think our generation would stoop to the same lows that they have. Well maybe somewhere in the future we won't have to make people decide. Maybe one day we will learn to indoctrinate all kids into a loving, caring, compassionate, and fairer society. Christy are we even allowed by law to be talking about what we are talking about? I don't know but let's change the subject and enjoy the rest of our movie night. We don't do this enough if you ask me. Yeah, Alan said, we should do this more often because who knows what tomorrow will bring. They both spent the next three hours watching their movies and enjoying each other's company. The summer finally arrived and again the family's celebrated both of the kids birthdays with their annual cookout and huge cake for dessert festivities. Alan and the rest of the band decided to skip band camp this summer and instead stay at home and enjoy each other's company and jam on their music together. They would stay up half of the night playing around talking about music, and now girls a lot. They would drink lemonade, and eat sugary snacks.

Christy would show up and they would just have a great time laughing and enjoying each other company as 15 year olds without a worry in the world. No one had to worry about having a roof over their head, shoes on their feet, and food on the table. None of the kids had to get summer jobs because all of their parents, as well as every family in their sector earned enough money to fully support their families. The summer was going along without a hitch until one day Alan got an email from Aaron his friend from band camp and ask Alan if he could come and visit him. Alan was a little taken back by the request and didn't know how to process it in his mind, so he turned to his best friend Christy for some advice. He told Christy about the email and ask her for her opinion about what he should do. Christy told him that if Aaron is your friend by all means invite him to come and visit for a couple of days. Just tell him two or three days, and no more. Alright Alan said I will invite him to visit for two days, but I don't know how the other band members would feel if they knew that Aaron was gay. Christy said you should give your friends more credit than you do maybe they would understand and feel the same way you do about other people's rights. Ok, well I will tell him that he is welcome than. So Alan emailed Aaron and ask him when he wanted to come and visit. Aaron said on a Thursday and that way when I leave on a Sunday there won't be a bunch of traffic and crowds at the airport. The fight is only 59 minutes from where Aaron lived at in Utah but still it could get crowded in the airport at certain time. So that following Thursday Aaron's parents let him get on a plane to go visit his friend Alan in Arizona. Upon arrival Alan introduced Aaron to his parents who were more than happy to allow Alan to have a friend come and visit for two days. Although Alan's parents didn't know Aaron was gay. They had no ideal about the shower incident at band camp. So Aaron arrived and Alan felt more uncomfortable then he thought he would. He realized that he would be sharing an adjoining bedroom with a boy that had a crush on him. Alan thought to himself can he handle this, or will he lose control and say, or do something that he would later regret. Aaron on the other hand was very lose and up for anything and glad that he got to get away from home for two or three days. His parents knew he was gay and they were a little overbearing about it sometimes. Aaron's parents didn't know about the camp shower incident, or that Aaron had a boy crush on Alan. Alan and Aaron decided to spend Aaron's first day in town with Christy watching movies, and just hanging out. Christy was happy meeting Aaron for the first time after hearing so much about him. Aaron told Christy that he was happy to meet her and had heard a lot of good things about her from Alan. Aaron told her that he felt like he knew her because of how much Alan talked about her. Christy told Aaron immediately that just so we are all comfortable why you are here Alan told me you are gay and I'm fine with that. Aaron with a bit of surprise on his face said ok, well I'm glad we got all of that out of the way. I appreciate that you don't judge me for what I am, and how I was born. Christy replied well enough pleasantries let's eat some popcorn, drink some cold drinks and watch some good movies. So the three of them watched movies and relaxed for the next four hours. The next day Alan went by himself to meet with his band members. He wanted to ask them in his own words how they felt about gay people. The reason why is that Aaron being a year older had started to exhibit tendencies that would let some people just by looking at the way he carries himself assume that he is gay. Alan didn't want to come right out and ask his friends how they felt about gay people so he had They all had met Aaron at band camp, but that was last year and Aaron's mannerisms have changed a lot. A little game of word association if we can call it that to find out. Alan quietly approached his friends who were sitting in (Milo's) one of his friends garages. Alan at first made small talk and then gingerly asked his friends how they felt about other people in general. Everyone looked perplexed and one of them ask Alan what he was getting at. Alan said I have a suggestion why don't we write down on a piece of paper what we don't like about other people, and what kind of people we don't like. They all smiled and said ok. So Alan picked up an old bowl that was lying around in the garage and ask everyone to write down their feelings in a short sentence or on word and put it in. So they all did, after ten minutes they were all finished writing and Alan took the pieces of paper out of the bowl and read them. Alan was totally shocked and thought did he really know these guys that he had grown up with, partied with, attended school with, and started a band with? The first piece of paper he read said I don't like Muslims, or anything related to Islam, the second piece of paper said I don't like rich people, the third said I tolerate them in my sector, and like some of them but I don't really like black people as a whole. The fourth piece of paper said I don't like Muslims, the fifth piece of paper said I don't like Jews, the sixth piece of paper said I don't like gay people, and the seventh piece of paper said I hate gay people, Muslims, and rich people. Alan was speechless, he looked at his friends and said are you guys serious, is this a joke, I have known you guys all of my life and I never knew that any of you felt this way. Ronnie and Payne the two black guys said that whichever one of you who doesn't like black people needs your ass whooped. One of the white guys named John said that we did this to see where we stand as far as our feelings go about society, and now that we know how we each feel let's not let this destroy our immediate friendship that we have as kids. We will all be sectoring in three short years anyway. So let's not ask each other who said what and get on with our live. Ronnie, and Payne said we both feel hurt that one of you doesn't like black people. Alan then replied, well what about everyone else do you two care that gays, and Muslims aren't liked either. So as long as it is not you it doesn't matter about dislike of hate. John responded that hate is too strong of a word to use. Ronnie asked John if he is the one that said he didn't like black people. John replied I'm not telling what I wrote, and if you guys are my true friends you will leave it at that, besides you two obviously don't like someone also so quit playing almighty. John said for all we know one of you could have said that you don't like black people who knows, and who cares at this young moment in our lives. Let's pretend that we give damn about each other and progress through the next three years of our lives, and then we probably will never have to see each other again. They all agreed that they would keep what they had just did to themselves and continue to be fun loving teenagers that they have always been. Alan told them that he had a friend in town visiting him so he would not be hanging out with them for a few days. John remarked why you don't bring this friend around to meet us. Alan said no we won't have time, he is only here for a few days and we have a lot planned. John said that doesn't sound like you to have a visitor and not want to hang out with us. Did the little paper game we just played offend you that much. Alan remarked that actually it did, and it's a good ideal for us to just chill of a couple of days and calm down. The other band members agreed it would be a good idea to get away from each other for a couple of days. Alan left the garage and returned home; Alan asked Aaron if he wanted to take in good restaurant, and just hang out with him and Christy and talk. Aaron said that sounds like a good ideal. So Aaron, Alan, and Christy went to a four star restaurant and ate a nice steak with all of the trimmings. Later on that night Aaron ask Alan, so when do I get to meet your friends? Alan with a perplexed look on his face said without being able to think about something to say fast so that he wouldn't hurt Aaron feelings said that you are only in town for a couple of days and I like your friendship I didn't want to face any of our time on my friends, we can see them anytime. I wanted to show you around the sites, and the mountains, and some other great things to see why you are here. Without giving it much thought Aaron said ok, that sounds great. They called it a day and turned in for a good night sleep. The next day Alan show Aaron a couple of the mountains where he and Christy like to go hiking at, and show him some famous sites in Scottsdale, and then they went to get some ice cream at a local ice cream parlor. Alan ask Aaron if he was having a good time. Aaron replied yes, this is great, I don't have a lot of good friends back at home. The older that I have gotten the more I have become a loner. Being gay I'm just biding my time until I turn 18 years old and can move to the Gay sector of the United States. There I won't be frightened all of the time about what ifs and maybes, I can finally be myself and quit putting on a fake face like I do now when I'm around friends, and at school. But I'm not scared of what people think at all anywhere. I keep thinking that although the laws to protect me are pretty strong that someone will still some day before I leave try to hurt me, or belittle me for who I am. Alan thought wow, I guess you have a good point, life is sometime hard my friend. You will always have a friend in me. I will never judge you, hurt you, or belittle you in anyway. I look at all people as equals, we all are born and we all will die. If someone dies and then comes back after being dead for around three weeks then I will certainly say that that person is a better person then I am. Aaron replied that is good to be here I feel very comfortable coming to here to visit. Are your friends as understanding as you are Alan. Alan again was at a loss for words, said I don't know and don't care I never asked them personal questions like that. Aaron thought ok, I think I hit a nerve I will leave it alone. Alan said I'm sorry I didn't mean to snap at you, Alan, knowing that he was lying just try to change the subject. Hey Aaron lets go see what Christy is doing today, Aaron said ok, lead the way. They went over to Christy house and found her in her back yard drinking ice cold lemonade and reading a book. Christy said with some excitement I glad you guys came over I was getting bored sitting here by myself. What have you two been up to? Alan said nothing much just talking and enjoying some ice cream. Christy said next time you guys go for ice cream you better invite me. Would you guys like some lemonade Christy asked? Yes they both said, and they all three spent the rest of the evening drinking lemonade and talking in Christy family's back yard. The next day Alan took Aaron to breakfast at Perkins restaurant buffet. While they were eating a couple of the members of the band just happened to be there eating breakfast also. They came over to the table that Alan and Aaron were sitting at and said good morning. John said hey isn't that one of the kids that we met at band camp last year. Aaron replied yes, I remember you guys and Alan of course you guys have a very good band. How come you came to visit Alan and you haven't come by to say what's up to any of the rest of us, you don't like us Aaron John ask laughing. John said I'm just kidding Aaron, how have you been? Is Alan showing you a good time, and all of the good things that Arizona has to offer? Yes, Alan is a very good host, and yes he has shown me some good sites. John ask when are you leaving Aaron. Alan chimed in and said that he is leaving tomorrow night. John said then you guys should come by Ronnie's house we are going to be jamming to some music and hanging out tonight. Ronnie parents are not going to be home all night so we have the place to ourselves. Since Ronnie lives on the edge of town there aren't a lot of neighbors to bother with loud music. Alan said ok, we will bring Christy with us also, it sounds like a lot of fun, and great way to give Aaron a sendoff from his visit. So later on that night after taking a nice naps the boys, along with Christy headed over to Ronnie house to hang out with their band friends. Upon arrival Alan noticed that there was about 35 people there. They were all milling around drinking cold lemonade, and eating finger sandwiches, and other snacks that Ronnie had prepared for the guests. Aaron asked Christy and Alan to introduce their some of their friends to him. Alan said ok, and in kind of a loud voice said everyone this is my friend Aaron from band camp. Some of you know him already because of course you attended band camp for a couple of years also. For those of you who don't know him he is here until tomorrow and Christy and I have been showing him our city, and some of the sites; so guys show him a good time and be nice to our guest. Everybody said welcome to Aaron and went back to milling around eating and drinking the refreshments. Ronnie asked the other band members to join him on a makeshift stage he had constructed in his parents back yard to play a couple of songs. They all said ok and proceeded to start playing, the other teenagers loved the music and began to sing along, and dance. Christy and Aaron found a couple of lawn chairs sit down and continued to watch the band perform. Aaron said these guys are good, and have improved since I heard them at band camp. Christy said I know they keep getting better and better, if they end up in the same life sector they are going to be really special, and make a lot of money becoming famous. Just then a girl that Christy knew from school named Janice asked Aaron if he wanted to dance. Aaron replied no, I'm not a very good dancer, maybe later. Janice said ok, I will ask you later. Janice asked Christy if she wanted to walk over to the refreshment table to get something to drink with her. Christy said sure, excused herself with Aaron and walked over to the refreshment table with Janice. Janice asked Christy if Aaron had a girlfriend, Christy got very nervous and said I don't know. I don't know Aaron that well he has only been here for a couple of days. I don't know him from band camp like the band guys do. Janice replied I think he is very cute, I'm going to ask him to dance again later on. Christy with her face turning a little red said good luck, Janice said good luck, why do you say good luck, Christy said awe no reason just making conversation with you. They both got big glasses of lemonade and headed back over to where Aaron was sitting and continued listening to the band play. Janice eventually walked away and started mingling with some of the other guest. Christy seizing the opportunity informed Aaron that Janice had a little crush on him. Aaron then asked Christy is she had informed her that he is gay. Christy responded no I didn't tell her that you are gay. I didn't really reply to her when she said that she liked you. Aaron said that I'm proud to be gay and if she asked me I will tell her that I'm indeed gay. Christy said Aaron I don't think that is a good ideal for you to tell her that you are gay. Although these people are school mates of mines, you know as well as I do that our sector is not a gay sector. Telling people you are gay is something that is reserved for when you pick your sector. I know that our laws are supposed to protect kids from any kind of violence, bigotry, or discrimination but these are teenagers who let their emotions get away from them sometimes regardless of the consequences. Aaron said I do have a legal protection and the punishment would be very harsh even for a teens if I were hurt in some way. Yes that is true Aaron but the law doesn't, and won't protect your feelings and the feeling of anger that you may endure. Aaron said you sound quite sure that your friends will not accept me, how can you be so sure. Well Aaron I don't know how everyone will act as a whole but I do know for a fact that one or two of these people have voiced their displeasure with gay people. Wow, I understand Christy but I'm not ashamed of who I am and I never will be. I don't care what people think, I used to be scared when I was younger but I'm not anymore. Christy said I will support you and stand by your side as your new friend, but I just want you to be careful. Aaron said I appreciate that, and thanks for being a friend. About ten minutes later Janice asked Aaron to dance. Aaron said it would be my pleasure to dance with you Janice. So they started dancing, two fast songs played and then a slow love song came on and Janice put her arms around Aaron and began slow dancing with him. Aaron felt very uncomfortable, but remembered that she ask and he said yes so just go with the flow he thought. At the end of the song Janice kissed him on his cheek and thanked him for dancing with her. She ask Aaron is he wanted to get some lemonade and he said sure, as they walked over to where the lemonade was Janice wrapped her arm around Aaron's arm and ask him if he had a girlfriend. Aaron replied no I don't have a girlfriend Janice. Janice then remarked so you haven't found the right girl yet, or are you just shy or something. Aaron said no Janice actually I'm gay, Janice said with a loud surprising voice your "GAY" Aaron said yes, and as he did a lot of the other kids stopped what they were doing because they had heard what Janice said and kind of started starring at Aaron. Janice who was completely embarrassed by the way she had just reacted said damn. A lot of the males at the party were looking at Aaron with anger, and disgust in their eyes. Alan overheard all of the commotion and went to find Christy. Once he found Christy; he said that he heard a lot of mumbling amongst the teenagers about gay people and their feelings toward them. It was most of the guys at the party doing the rumbling. Alan said maybe we should get Aaron and leave, Christy said ok, but I'm not too worried, everyone here knows that there are very stiff penalties for attacking someone before they become an adult and choose a sector of life. Alan said you are right, but who knows what teenagers are capable of. Just then as they were walking toward Aaron and Janice that loud mouth kid named John said Damn Alan if I knew you were going to bring a faggot I wouldn't have asked you to come. Christy and Alan immediately said John you are out of line, and then Ronnie chirped in and said that he is not out of line this is why we have sectors I too don't like faggots. Aaron fuming now said the hell with both of you I will be out of people like you two's hair soon enough. John said the quicker the better, I think all fags are going to hell anyway. Alan said John that's enough, and told Aaron let's get out of here. One of the other kids at the party spoke up and said that I will be applying to leave the United States when I turn 18 years old to be with my Muslim brothers, and sisters; and under my new religions laws you would be stoned to death Aaron, or thrown off of a building for being a faggot. Just then about nine or ten of the other kids said if you are going to be a Muslim you are no better than the fags. You towel heads caused 9/11 and are the reason why we even have sectors that split families up you want to be murdering, suicidal bastard. A couple of other teens then shouted that they hated niggers, and that it is their fault because of how lazy, and criminalistic they are that we have sectors. Some else shouted that wetbacks from Mexico had invaded the country and tried to turn it into a third world country. Another teen shouted no, my dad said it's because the Jewish kikes sucked up all of the money and turned everyone against each other that we have sectors. After the Jew comment was made fist started flying from every direction, blacks fighting whites, whites fighting whites, and a group of teens who went straight after Aaron, and the teen who said that he wanted to be a Muslim. Christy and Alan tried to get over to Aaron through the mass of people. They could see Aaron being pummeled with fist and kicks flying from all directions. The kid who said that he wanted to be a Muslim broke loose from the beating the beating he was taking and ran down the street screaming. By the time Christy and Alan made their way over to Aaron he was bloodied and unconscious laying on the ground still being kicked by a couple of teens shouting die faggot. Christy threw herself on top of him in an attempt to stop the savage beating from continuing. Alan was screaming at the teens that he knew to stop fighting and calm down. After about two minutes of fighting everyone started calming down as far as throwing punches. Teens were still hurdling verbal insults at each other laced with racism, anti-sematic furor. At last the police showed up in droves because of course there are video cameras everywhere and this was reported by the watch group who monitors the video to the United States Police. The police surrounded the party of teens so that no one could leave, then they brought in paramedics to help the teens like Aaron who were badly hurt. Alan was screaming at all of the teens saying that I grew up with you guys, we have partied together, spent time with each other's family's, we go to the same schools, and live in the same neighborhood what the hell happened, how did we get to this point in our lives? One of the teens shouted what happened is that we grew up, welcome to the real world my friend, welcome to the real world. The Police after getting all 15 of the wounded and hurt teenagers into ambulances that were beaten asked the video control center to rewind the video and tell them who the aggressors were in the fight. After playing back the video the police ended up arresting 16 teenagers for assault and a couple were charged with felonious assault for the beating that they laid on Aaron. Christy and Alan weren't charged and were later released to their parents who had to come and pick them up at the police station. Alan, and Christy explained to their parents how this whole fiasco started and asked if they could go to the hospital to visit Aaron. Their parents said yes and drove them to the hospital to visit their badly beaten friend. Aaron was awake and alert and talking to his parents on the telephone when Christy and Alan arrived at the hospital to visit him. Aaron immediately after he finished talking to his parents told Christy and Alan I was wrong for telling your friends that I'm gay. Christy immediately disagreed with him saying that your sexuality is your business, but for someone to dislike you for it and want to hurt you is their hang up. Aaron ask what happened after he was rendered unconscious. Alan answered that there were some sporadic fighting that went on after you were unconscious for about two minutes until everyone calmed down and the police showed up. Aaron told them that the doctor said he would be in the hospital for a couple of days so they could monitor his concussion that he had gotten during the assault. Alan said I'm sorry you came to visit and you end up in the hospital. Christy said jokingly other than the assault, how do you like our city? Aaron laughed back and said I'm glad that I at least made two great friends like you two. They talked for another two hours before Alan and Christy parents said it was time to go home and let Aaron rest up. The next day detectives from the Police Department came to pay Alan, and Christy a visit and ask them what started this whole thing. Christy said discrimination and stupidity is the cause of it, Alan agreed. They both told detectives that Aaron was their guest and that he is a nice kid that got beat up for being gay. Detectives took their statements and gave them a court day when they along with the other 30 or 35 kids would have to appear in what is called a justice forum. Until the justice forums you are not allowed to talk to or go around any of the other kids that were at the party, except for Aaron. The justice forum was set for next week on a Tuesday morning. On the day of the justice forum Alan and Christy parents sit them down a couple of hours before the forum and explained to them that they were in for a rude surprise as far a breaking the law went in there sector. The criminal Justice system is nowhere what it used to years ago like what you two have seen on videos in school. The new sectored justice system is a lot more disciplined and right to the point about what sectors consider crime to be and how to deal with it. Alan and Christy were now very scared although they had done nothing wrong. When they arrived at the Justice center they were seated away from all of the other teens. All of the teens involved in this fracas were separated and only allowed to sit with their parents if they chose to do so. The teens that had been arrested were brought in from the juvenile detention center and also not allowed to sit together. In the sectors the administrators are not called Judges, they are called Sector Lords. There is none of the past decorum like all rise, or how do you plea, or an initial appearance, or lawyers that represent clients. The Sector Lord is the only one who does any talking and deciding what is going to happen. The Sector Lords are not elected officials, they are chosen, and then receive lifelong appointments based on their education. You must have obtained a Ph.D. to be a Sector Lord from a U.S Accredited University. The Sector Lord said I will now pronounce sentence. There will be no testimony, and there will be no outburst in the Justice Forum. Is that understood by everyone, in unison everyone said yes Lord. I sentence all of the kids that were arrested to three months of detainment in the juvenile human hold center. All other juveniles, and the juveniles sentenced to the juvenile human hold center will be indoctrinated at age 16 into sectors of life. A loud gasp went out from all of the teens, a lot of them especially the girls started sobbing uncontrollably, and shaking their heads. The Sector Lord immediately said silence, silence, wipe your eyes and shut up. All the kids immediately complied not wanting more punishment. The punishment meant that all of these kids would lose two years of life with their family's for their actions. They can of course visit, but not living there and having to be on your own at age 16 is a crazy punishment. Welcome to the new world the Sector Lord proclaimed. Alan and Christy thinking that wow what a harsh punishment for their friends. They looked at each other with looks of almost. One of the other teens said I don't know what you two are gawking about this means you too. Christy, and Alan didn't think that this meant them to. So they waited until the proceedings were over and asked, and to their utter amazement it did mean them too. They asked what they had done wrong only to be told that because of U.S law if they were not sectored out or in that there could potentially be problems with other teens family's so in cases like this it is best to send everyone to an early sector life to keep the peace. Also none of the kids would be able to return to their current high school to finish their last year, but instead would be broken up amongst internet schools and other outlying schools so there would be little or no contact at all amongst all of the teens involved in the fracas, even the teens who just watched and did not take part in throwing punches, or kicking someone. Alan and Christy were horrified; Christy cried all the way home, and all night long. How could I lose two years of my life with my family for diving on a boy being beaten at a party? The next day Alan and Christy sit down with their parents and asked them if there was anything they could do to avoid this. Their parents said the only way to avoid this is to pass your polygraph test saying that you want to live in this sector and then it won't matter about an early exit out of high school and into a sector. Christy was fine with this and thought that this maybe indeed the sector for her, but Alan knew in his heart that there was no way that he could pass a polygraph test for this sector. Alan went to dinner with Christy and at dinner told her that they were going to just have to accept this part of their lives. Alan said I will try to spend as much time with you and my parents as I can over the next year. Where ever I end up there is always skype and visitation with our families, so it's not like we will never see each other again. Yeah Christy said I should look at the bright side of life, but it still won't be the same like it is now. I guess this is what growing up is all about. Alan asked Christy if she wanted to go drowned their sorrows over some ice cream and then take in a movie. She said yes, so off they went that night. First to the local yogurt shop for some yogurt and then off to the movie to see a comedy/chick flick. Christy and Aland had a long talk on their way home from the movies about their current situation and the year to come. Christy asked Alan if he thought their punishment for doing nothing was fair. Alan said no, but we did take Aaron to the party so we are a little complicit in what happened. But I don't think we should be punished so harshly. It sounds like the Government does things one way and one way only. They were finally home and Alan said good night and started walking toward his home when out of the shadows jumped John one of the band members and someone who has known Alan all of his life. He in the blink of an eye produced a large bowie knife and stabbed Alan repeatedly in the back and chest area. Alan fell to the ground screaming in agony from the pain. Alan's parents, and Christy and her parents along with several other neighbors heard Alan's screams and ran to out to help him. Christy held Alan's hand and asked who had did this to him? Alan in a shaking fading voice said it was John. Alan's parents phoned paramedics and they came and rushed Alan to the hospital but it was too late Alan was gone. Christy couldn't believe it her best friend gone in an instant. Christy was in shock for three days, but knew she had to pull it together for Alan's funeral on that Friday. Christy asked Alan's parents if she could give the eulogy at Alan's funeral. Alan's parents gladly said yes, we have always considered you to be Alan's sister and our daughter.

Alan's parents and everyone that knew him were devastated. John was subsequently arrested and sentenced to death to be carried out immediately. So actually two young lives have been lost over senseless violence. Alan's death took place on a Monday, and his funeral is scheduled for Friday of the same week. Aaron was the first to say a few words before Christy gave the eulogy; Alan was a very understanding person and very mature for his age, his kind of kindness is what society needs. Christy then gave Alan's eulogy which she said what is the use of having sectors if these types of incidents still take place? Christy said choking back tears the entire speech, what does it take for human beings to be human, what does it take for humans to have compassion in our hearts? How can we as a race of people continue to thrive if we hurt, maim, and kill each other over labels? Christy closed by saying I love you Alan and always will, God bless us all.

The End

Conclusion/Imagination

The society that this book just described in a lure of fantasy and non-sense is not really non sense when you think about the fact that we have had several societies that have tried to do these very things. Hitler tried it and almost succeeded, Rome actually had an empire so vast at one time that the sun never set on their empire, America with slavery of blacks, and countless other societies that I would need to write another book about too explain. I'm always amazed when people say that we are different based on religion, or gender, or race, or economics, or any other class that we can categorize ourselves in. But we are all born the exact same way, the egg is fertilized by the semen or seed as we call it, and then about nine months later a baby girl, or boy pops out. There is no other category's you are either a girl, or boy or both. There is no other category that exists as we know it. Here's the kicker we all need food and water to live, we all need oxygen to breath, and we all will eventually die until someone figures out how to escape that. We all normally urinate, crap, blow our noses, walk, talk, sleep with our eyes closed, and make love. It doesn't matter where you are born at on the planet if you are human you normally do these things, or need these things. It doesn't matter how much education, money, big or little houses, or cars you drive you still need water and food to continue to survive as a human being on this planet. These are the foundational aspects of life. Everything else is given, taken, indoctrinated, brain washed in, learned, taught, or grabbed out of something we call life. . If our society doesn't change this is exactly what kind of society that we are headed toward. Only love and an open mind toward others will save us from this fantasy reality. We don't need racism, ageism, fascism, mentalism, classism, sexism, or any other kind of ism to survive and flourish as a human beings. Since we don't need any of these things to survive and exist why we kill each other, start wars, and separate, indoctrinate, brainwash, and create all other kinds of nonsense to get ourselves into the frame of mind with these things. We should be so engrossed in being who we are in our uniqueness and in love with ourselves so much that we don't want to, or even have time to worry about or go hurt other people. We no more need isms then we do a pink rock, there is just no common sense use or great good as a human beings that will be achieved because of them, so please give them up. If you believe in heaven than common sense should tell us that none of these things exist there. My name is Phillip a label that I actually accept; thank you very much for reading my short book, now please go drink a cold glass of lemonade, eat Twinkies, apple pie, be happy, smile, make love, laugh and enjoy life to its fullest without hurting other people.